Exploring the Ancient World

THE AZTEC EMPIRE

Robert Hull

Gareth Stevens
Publishing

Please visit our Web site, www.garethstevens.com. For a free color catalog of all our high-quality books, call toll free 1-800-542-2595 or fax 1-877-542-2596.

Library of Congress Cataloging-in-Publication Data

Hull, Robert, 1935-
The Aztec empire / Robert Hull.
    p. cm. — (Exploring the ancient world)
Includes index.
 ISBN 978-1-4339-4161-0 (library binding)
1. Aztecs—Juvenile literature. 2. Aztecs—History—Juvenile literature.
3. Aztecs—Social life and customs—Juvenile literature. I. Title.
F1219.73.H848 2011
972—dc22

2010014428

This edition first published in 2011 by
Gareth Stevens Publishing
111 East 14th Street, Suite 349
New York, NY 10003

Copyright © 2011 Wayland/Gareth Stevens Publishing

Editorial Director: Kerri O'Donnell
Art Director: Haley Harasymiw

Photo Credits:
Ronald Sheridan, Ancient Art and Architecture Collection Ltd 37, 41 (R. Sterling), 54; E. T. Archive front cover (right), 7, 14 (Bib. Nac. Mexico), 16 (Antochiw Collection), 18, 20, 23 (Templo Mayor Museum, Mexico City), 25 (Museo Ciudad Mexico/ Sapicha), 43 (National Palace, Mexico), 48 (Antochiw Collection), 49 (British Museum, London), 53 (top), 53 (bottom—Antochiw Collection), 57 (right); Mexicolore 8, 13, 15, 22, 45; Shutterstock *cover* and 1 (Dwight Smith); Tony Morrison, South American Pictures 10, 28, 31, 40, 57 (Chris Sharp), 59; Werner Forman Archive 5 (top—Museum fur Volkerkunde, Vienna), 5 (bottom); 6 (Anthropology Museum, Veracruz University, Jalapa), 11, 17, (British Museum, London), 19 (Museum fur Volkerkunde, Vienna), 24, 26 (National Museum of Anthropology, Mexico City), 27 (National Museum of Anthropology, Mexico City), 30 (Museum fur Volkerkunde, Basel), 32 (Liverpool Museum, Liverpool), 33 (Museo Nazionale Preistorico Etnografico Luigi Pigoroni, Rome), 34 (Museum fur Volkerkunde, Basel), 35 (National Museum of Anthropology, Mexico City), 38 (British Museum, London), 39 (National Museum of Anthropology, Mexico City), 44 (British Museum, London), 46 (Museum fur Volkerkunde, Vienna), 47 (Liverpool Museum, Liverpool), 51 (top), 51 (bottom), 55 (National Museum of Anthropology, Mexico City), 60 (N. J. Saunders). Map artwork: Peter Bull

Printed in China
CPSIA compliance information: Batch #WAS10GS: For further information contact Gareth Stevens, New York, New York at 1-800-542-2595.

Contents

The Aztec Story

Europeans Come to Mexico

In 1519 CE, Hernando Cortés sailed from Cuba to Mexico. He was the commander of a Spanish expedition to find gold. He landed on the east coast, in Vera Cruz—its later Spanish name—with about 400 soldiers. He had no idea that he had landed at the edge of one of the most powerful empires in the world, or that its capital was only 125 mi. (200 km) away in the Valley of Mexico. Within just two years, Cortés and his few conquistadores (meaning "conquerors") had destroyed the Aztec empire and most of its civilization.

Knowledge About the Aztecs

We know a lot about the Aztecs from their records and from the memoirs of the conquering Spaniards. Cortés wrote letters to the King of Spain about his adventures, and one of his soldiers, Bernal Diaz, wrote down his memories of the Conquistadores' campaigns. The Aztecs painted their records in books, called codices, including information about their gods, history, laws, customs, and daily life. The codices were painted on strips of deerskin, bark, or agave paper.

▼ *This map shows the region where the Aztecs lived. This part of North and South America is called Mesoamerica and includes Central America and much of modern Mexico.*

FROM ASIA

NORTH AMERICA

ATLANTIC OCEAN

Teotihuacan

Chichen Itza

Tenochtitlan

Tikal

Monte Alban

PACIFIC OCEAN

SOUTH AMERICA

Aztec

Maya

Route of migration

This codex shows two war chiefs talking. We can see, from his downturned hand—a sign of submission—that the one on the left is giving himself up to the other. When Cortés and his followers moved inland, the leaders of the many Mexican tribes must have sat in meetings to discuss tactics just like this one.

The pictures do not represent words; they are illustrations of thoughts or ideas. When the codices were "read" aloud, the reader added his own interpretation of the story. In this way, knowledge was passed on by word of mouth, with the painted books to prompt the memory. Unfortunately, during the Spanish conquest, priests burned many of these precious *codices* because they showed stories of non-Christian gods. Only a few survived, and some of these are thought to be copies made just after the conquest.

These surviving records tell us a great deal about Aztec life and the Spanish conquest of Mexico. There are also artifacts, or objects, that survive: terrifying stone sculptures, wooden drums, ruins of majestic temples, and fabulous jewelry made of gold and precious stones. Some priceless objects, which were stolen from the Aztecs during the Spanish invasion, were shipped back to Europe and can now be seen in museums. Although some Aztec objects have survived, thousands of examples of their craft have been destroyed, melted down, or lost.

When Cortés landed in Mexico, he was just south of Cempoala and Vera Cruz. As the Spanish sailed along the coast of Mexico, they stopped to visit many of the local cities and realized that the stories of a land rich in gold were true.

Mesoamerica
Before the Aztecs

Before the Aztecs

The Aztecs were not the first civilization of Mexico; other civilizations had come and gone in the high upland valley and along the coasts of Mexico a long time before them. They handed down to the Aztecs a lot of what we think of as Aztec culture: farming, gods, architecture, and customs. The story of these civilizations goes back even before 30,000 BCE, when people first entered North America from Asia. ("Indians" was the name later given to Native Americans by Columbus, who thought he was in the East Indies).

These early people eventually moved south, into the beautiful Valley of Mexico. This was a fertile land, with a fine climate. Many wandering groups settled around its lake, Lake Texcoco. By about 3500 BCE, a kind of corn was being cultivated; this was the first sign of agriculture. By 2000 BCE, people were building wattle and daub houses, and making clay pottery. By 1500 BCE, a kind of floating garden, called a *chinampa*, was being used to grow food.

The Olmecs

Between about 1000 and 300 BCE, the people along the coast of the Caribbean began living in small cities. These civilized people were called the Olmecs. They built

▼ *Nobody is sure what this giant Olmec head represents. It must have had some significance in Olmec society. The heads all show men with fleshy faces, wearing tight-fitting caps.*

pyramid temples 100 ft. (30 m) high, with mosaics and huge sculptures. Their priests drew hieroglyphics and studied the stars, and there were very sophisticated painters.

The Olmecs were the first society to develop a system of religious leadership. Their priests were the leaders of the people and made all the important decisions.

The Maya

The Maya made up another early civilization in Mesoamerica. By the second century CE, they had become very skilled artists and architects. They made wonderful stone carvings and painted books on bark paper. The wealth of the society was such that some aristocrats even filled their teeth and had them inlaid with precious stones to show how important they were.

By the fourth century CE, the Maya were living in large cities. They built houses with steam baths and towns with paved avenues, open squares, and underwater drainage systems.

The Maya were also excellent mathematicians. Their intellectuals invented the idea of "zero" and had accurate calendars. These were necessary to forecast the agricultural seasons—as the population grew, crops became essential to feed everyone. Mayan kings declared war on their neighbors, and human sacrifices took place, too, but not on the enormous scale that it did later under the Aztecs.

▲ All of the surfaces of the Mayan temple-cities were highly decorated with flamboyant designs of mythical monsters and religious symbols. This stone work shows the head of the god Quetzalcoatl, which has been carved into one of the temples at Teotihuacan.

Priests were the most powerful people in the Mayan world; they dressed in golden jaguar skins, blood-red robes, and headdresses with feathers from the vivid-green Quetzal bird. The most ancient god was Tlaloc the rain god, and the most powerful god was Quetzalcoatl, the Feathered Serpent—both of these gods were adopted by Aztec religion later.

In the tenth century CE, Mayan civilization suddenly and mysteriously collapsed. Their beautiful cities were abandoned, and the people began to live in small farming communities.

Teotihuacan

At the time the Maya were flourishing, in the high plateau of Mesoamerica the Toltecs were building a civilization that would inspire the cultural and artistic development of Mesoamerica. Teotihuacan, their great city, flourished between 200 and 700 CE. In later times, the Aztecs made pilgrimages to the ruins of Teotihuacan and called it the "City of the Gods." It was the first big Mesoamerican city; it spread over more than 7 sq. mi. (18 sq. km) and it was planned in a gridwork pattern. There were more than 2,000 major buildings, including temples, palaces, markets, and apartments.

▼ *The Aztecs believed that the Pyramid of the Sun was where the sun had been born. It is four times bigger than the pyramid of Cheops in Egypt. It was built on top of a smaller pyramid in the second century BCE. It stands in the middle of the 2-mile (3.2-km)-long "Avenue of the Dead"—a great avenue of religious buildings that became the center of the city of Teotihuacan.*

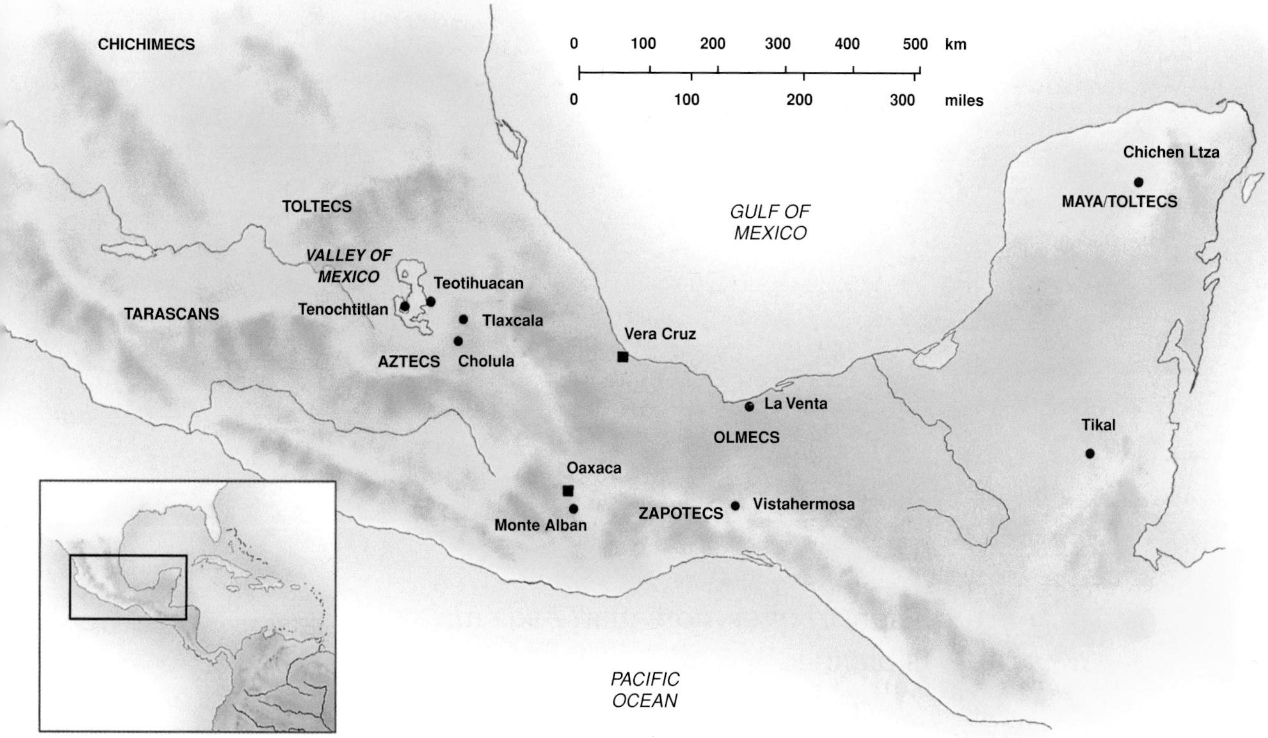
CHICHIMECS
0 100 200 300 400 500 km
0 100 200 300 miles
Chichen Ltza
MAYA/TOLTECS
TOLTECS
GULF OF MEXICO
VALLEY OF MEXICO
Teotihuacan
TARASCANS
Tenochtitlan
Tlaxcala
Vera Cruz
AZTECS
Cholula
La Venta
OLMECS
Tikal
Oaxaca
Monte Alban
ZAPOTECS
Vistahermosa
PACIFIC OCEAN

▲ ***This map shows where each of the different pre-Aztec civilizations was based.***

The pyramids built by the Maya and the Aztecs were somewhat similar to the ones built by the Egyptians. However, although these ancient Mexican civilizations came later than the Egyptians, they knew nothing about the Egyptian civilization in Africa. Unlike Egyptian pyramids, the stepped pyramids of ancient Mexico had temples at the summit. Also, the Mexican pyramids were not always used as tombs, but also as places of worship.

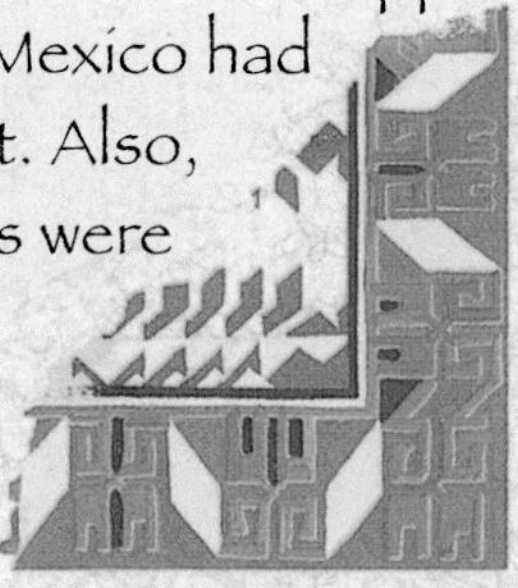

Two great pyramids stand opposite each other in the "Avenue of the Dead": the Pyramid of the Sun and the smaller Pyramid of the Moon. One statue found there, of the rain god Tlaloc, weighs 170 tons and was cut from a single stone. Next to these temples is a third, dedicated to the god Quetzalcoatl.

In 650 CE, Teotihuacan was destroyed, probably by Chichimecs. These were fierce nomadic tribes from northern Mexico, who seized land to build military empires on. Many other cities fell into ruin around the same time. Nobody knows exactly why. The result of the destruction of the city of Teotihuacan was a 300-year collapse in Mesoamerican civilization.

Tula

After about 900 CE, the cities of Mesoamerica seem to have become more warlike. The Toltecs dominated most of this area between 900 CE and 1170 CE. Their priests were priest-warriors, who led their people into wars of conquest. Tula was the capital city of the Toltecs and another great city that the Aztecs admired. They called the age of the Toltecs "The Golden Age." Tula was a wealthy city; its palace rooms were decorated with the woven plumage of rare birds and sheets of gold and jewels. But it was a warlike and fierce civilization that lived within the city; its giant statues of warriors are grim and strong. The main temple at Tula was supported by stone columns carved into the images of warriors, and human sacrifice was practiced. A lot of information about the Toltecs was preserved in memorized Aztec poems, which were written down after the Spanish conquest. The Aztecs believed that the Toltecs had invented painting, sculpture, and picture writing. The ruins of Tula still stand, 60 mi. (96 km) northwest of Mexico City.

The Toltec world crumbled away in the twelfth century CE. Drought and famine had been threatening the Toltecs, and then Tula itself was destroyed about 1160 CE. The reasons for the collapse of this civilization are unclear, but other civilizations such as the Mixtecs flourished during this period.

▲ *The ballgame* ollama *was played in ancient Mesoamerica, on a special ball court with two or three players on each side, and a hard, heavy, rubber ball. The idea of the game was to hit the ball onto markers at the end of the court or up through a high stone ring. The players wore padding and could use various parts of their bodies to hit the ball: their upper arms, hips, or thighs. It was played so fiercely that it was almost a battle, not a game. Losing captains might even be sacrificed.*

Inspiration for the Aztecs

The civilizations of the Olmecs and the Maya were very different, but they had certain things in common that were later adopted by the Aztecs and absorbed into their society. They both built pyramid temples, and long, stone structures (two stands facing each other with an alley between), where they played a kind of ballgame called *ollama*. All of the pre-Aztec peoples seem to have had similar religious ideas and worshiped some of the same gods. They all used a calendar of 260 days and had similar beliefs about how their world was made.

▼ *These fierce-looking warriors came from Tula, where they were part of a supporting colonnade leading toward the central Pyramid of Quetzalcoatl. Firebirds, which were the symbols of the Toltec ruling class, are carved onto their chests.*

One story about Quetzalcoatl was that he fled from the Toltec city of Tula, promising to return in the year Ce Atl. So, when Cortés arrived in 1519 CE, the year Ce Atl, the Aztecs believed that their Tula predecessors had been right and Quetzalcoatl had arrived!

The Rise of Aztec Power

The Early History

In Aztec legends their original home was Aztlan, "The Place of Reeds." This was probably somewhere in northwest Mexico. The Aztecs left this place in 1168 CE and wandered for many years. At one stage they also settled for a while at Coatepec, "The Hill of the Snake." Here the sun god Huitzilopochtli, or "Hummingbird of the South," was born. They continued to search for a homeland until they arrived in the northern part of Central Mexico, some time after 1200 CE. They were then called the Mexica, pronounced "mesheeka." They traveled around in an area of the Mexican high plain, in the land around Lake Texcoco, until they moved to Chapultepec in the middle of the thirteenth century CE.

Eventually, they entered the Valley of Mexico, where they persuaded Coxcoxtli, ruler of Culhuacan, to give them land. He reluctantly gave them some infertile territory in a small valley infested with rattlesnakes. Land was scarce in the valley, and though the Aztecs were useful as paid fighters, they were not made welcome as settlers.

▼ *This map shows a possible route that the Aztecs may have taken on their wanderings. There is not a lot of information about the early part of their journey, but once they reached Chapultepec, there are plenty of records to tell us the route the Aztecs took.*

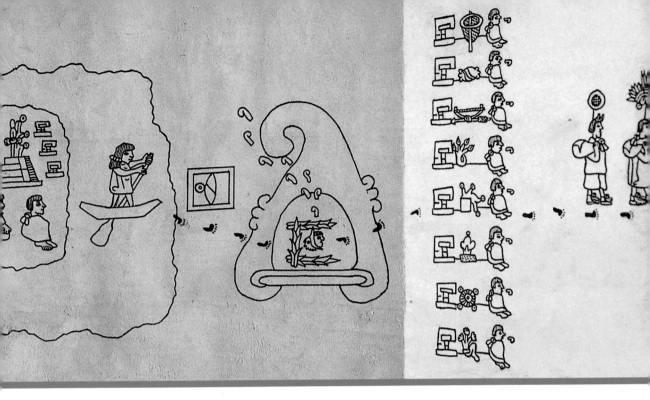

▲ *The* **Codex Boturini** *shows the Aztec journey from the mythical land of Aztlan to Tenochtitlan. The footprints trace the route that they took on their long journey. Historians think that the legend of the Aztec origins was possibly just a story made up by their leaders to hide their humble origins.*

They fought in wars for Coxcoxtli to prove their loyalty and skill as warriors. To show their successes they presented the Culhuacan leaders with a large basket filled with 8,000 enemy ears.

The Aztecs asked Coxcoxtli to send his daughter to be honored as their queen and goddess. Coxcoxtli agreed and went to the ceremony. He arrived to see that his daughter had been skinned alive, and a priest was dancing in her skin. In fury, the leaders of Culhuacan drove the Aztecs from their valley, into the lakeside marshes and onto a small, desolate island.

The story of the princess seems very barbaric to us now; but the Aztecs were equally horrified by some of the habits of the Spanish who invaded in the sixteenth century. Many refined Aztec nobles apparently put scented flowers to their noses when Spaniards went by, because they felt that the Spaniards did not wash frequently enough.

▲ *This scene from the* **Codex Aubin** *shows an eagle sitting on a cactus, with a snake in its beak.* **These symbols show the place where the Aztecs founded the city of Tenochtitlan.**

"The Place of the Cactus"

Once again the Aztecs were homeless. But the priests knew that Huitzilopochtli had decreed that they must finally settle where they saw an eagle with a snake in its grip sitting on a cactus. In 1325 CE, the Aztecs took refuge on a previously uninhabited, marshy island on the western tip of Lake Texcoco. They founded their home where they saw the sign that the gods had promised them. They began to build their new city. Tenochtitlan was founded in 1325 or 1345 CE, on this small island in Lake Texcoco. The site is now buried under Mexico City, the capital of modern-day Mexico. The island was gradually extended. Marshy areas were filled in with soil and rocks, and the lakeshore was dredged for mud. Offshore land was created by driving poles down into the lake bottom and creating wickerwork enclosures. Over time, these were filled in and built up.

An island city had many advantages for the Aztecs. One was defense, because invading soldiers could not march overland; they could approach the island only from the three causeways connecting with the mainland. Another was transportation, since it was easier to carry goods by canoe than to use the usual methods of transport—men and women carriers. The peoples of the Valley did not use animals or wheels for carrying goods; people carried goods on their backs. It seems strange that the Aztecs did not use the wheel or animals to carry goods, when they were so sophisticated in other ways, for example, in building techniques.

The Empire Develops

Tenochtitlan grew and grew, absorbing other smaller islands close to its shore. The power of Tenochtitlan grew as well. Its people learned to play one city off against another, perhaps through their trading skills.

The new island-dwellers had plenty of food, fish, and waterfowl especially. In their canoes the Aztecs traded fish, ducks, frogs, and other lake products with nearby cities.

For a while they were taken over and ruled by Tezozomoc, the fierce ruler of the Tepanecs. They then fought with the Tepanecs against Texcoco, the great city on the eastern side of the lake. After they were defeated, the people of Texcoco paid tribute directly to the Aztecs at Tenochtitlan. The Aztecs had begun building their empire. They now had control over other tribes and an income from the "tribute" or payments from conquered cities.

▼ *The three main causeways connecting Tenochtitlan to the mainland were to carry troops and supplies. There were gaps on each causeway. These were normally filled by huge pieces of timber, but in wartime the timber was rolled away, preventing enemy armies from reaching Tenochtitlan.*

The Emperors

Itzcoatl was the Aztec ruler from 1426 CE. He wanted to break free of the Tepanecs. When he refused to pay tribute to them, the Tepanecs blockaded Tenochtitlan. Itzcoatl then made an alliance with the Texcocoans, on the east shore of the lake, and Tlacopan, to the west of the lake. The Texcocoan leader Nezahualcoyotl then won the support of other cities, and together with the Aztecs they defeated the empire of the Tepanecs. In 1440 CE, Itzcoatl's nephew, Montezuma I, was elected Aztec leader. Under him the empire grew even faster.

But, in the middle of the fifteenth century CE, there were several agricultural disasters, and the small empire almost collapsed. In 1446, locusts ruined the harvest, and there was famine. Then, in 1449, after heavy snow and rain in the mountains, the lake level rose; fields disappeared under water and the city was flooded. From 1450 to 1454, frost killed the crops, and many people died or fled the area. Many others sold themselves into slavery to escape starvation.

▲ *Of all the gods of ancient Mexico, Huitzilopochtli, shown here in the* **Codex Florentine,** *was one of the most greedy for human blood. At the height of the Aztec empire, thousands of victims were sacrificed to him.*

According to legend, Huitzilopochtli had a human mother who became pregnant by holding a ball of feathers to her chest—it was a divine pregnancy. Her other children were angry and tried to kill her, but just as they did, Huitzilopochtli sprang from her womb, fully grown. He killed the hostile children.

During this period many more victims than normal were sacrificed, to calm the gods' anger. The rains of 1455 produced a huge harvest, and to the Aztecs it seemed that their willingness to sacrifice themselves had won them the favors of the gods. The apparent success of such large-scale sacrifice was an important lesson to the Aztecs and one that they lived by from then on.

The empire continued to grow. Montezuma I ordered the attack on other cities and villages on the lake. The Aztecs attacked cities on the north, south, and east of the Valley of Mexico. Tribute flowed in from all the subdued peoples, making Tenochtitlan even wealthier.

◀ *Chalchiuhtlicue, "Lady Precious Green," was a fertility goddess and an escort to Tlaloc, the god of rain. During droughts or floods, when food was in short supply, offerings were made to Tlaloc. If they were accepted, Tlaloc would send water to fertilize the earth.*

The Aztec Empire

Ahuitzotl

In 1490 CE, after Montezuma I died, Ahuitzotl took power. He led his army on long expeditions, conquering more peoples and expanding the empire. He is said to have taken 100,000 prisoners in his life.

When Ahuitzotl decided to build a great new temple to Huitzilopochtli, 20,000 victims were sacrificed in the dedication ceremonies: four columns of them, each stretching in a 3-mi. (5-km)-long line from the foot of the temple steps. Guests from other cities were invited to watch the ceremonies, to see for themselves the strength of the Aztec empire. From this time on, the Aztecs ruled through terror. Human sacrifice resulted in the spilling of huge amounts of human blood, to keep the gods on the side of the Aztec people.

► *This scene, from the* **Codex Magliabecchiano,** *shows a human sacrifice. In ceremonies like this, the victim would be pushed backward over a stone of sacrifice and held down by priests. Another priest then plunged a razor-sharp obsidian knife into the man's chest. This picture shows the victim's soul flying out of his chest, up to the gods. The symbol of the quetzal bird on the left of the picture suggests that the sacrifice was being made to the god Quetzalcoatl.*

The Triple Alliance

To gather victims, and to extend the lands of the empire, three cities of Mesoamerica combined in warfare: Tenochtitlan, Texcoco, and Tlacopan. This Triple Alliance received tribute from conquered cities. Tlacopan received a fifth, while Tenochtitlan and Texcoco got two-fifths each. The conquered cities paid fixed amounts on fixed dates. Each year Tenochtitlan received 7,000 tons of corn, 4,000 tons each of beans, chia seeds, and grain, an unbelievable 2 million cotton cloaks, and a huge quantity of war costumes, shields, and feather headdresses.

▲ *This beautiful feather-work shield may have been the ceremonial shield of the emperor Ahuitzotl. His name means "the water beast" and the picture shows a water beast with a knife in its mouth. The shield is outlined in gold.*

The life of Aztec priests was very strict. A priest had to follow certain rituals over many years before he was thought to be holy enough to be able to perform sacrifices to the gods. Often he would go through long periods of fasting, only living on three tortillas and a bowl of water a day. After many years, the priest reached the highest office and was able to perform human sacrifices. His work was expected to be precise and the heart had to be removed by a single slash of the knife. The sacrificing priest was very well respected by the Aztecs, because he was said to have a close relationship with the gods.

Aztec Rule

The Aztec empire was not like the Roman Empire. The Aztecs did not conquer and settle in distant regions; nor did they try to govern or reeducate the cities they had won in battle. The emperor simply required tribute: payment in goods and objects that would help keep the Aztecs wealthy and prosperous.

The imperial city of Tenochtitlan was too large to be self-sufficient and relied on tribute to buy essential supplies. Aztec codices show the tribute paid to Montezuma II, who was elected as ruler in 1502 CE.

One page shows the tribute due twice a year, from the six towns of the province of Xilotepec: women's skirts and blouses, men's clothing, warriors' dress with shields, one eagle, and four crates of beans, corn, and other food.

The Aztecs were not all-powerful; neither the Tlaxcalans nor the Tarascans were ever conquered by the Aztecs. There remained hostile cities within the Aztec empire. The Tlaxcalans, tired of being raided for sacrificial victims, supplied the Spanish with thousands of troops to fight against the hated Aztecs in 1519 CE. The Aztec empire was also weakened by the fact that some cities were linked only to Tenochtitlan by marriages, and it was only their fear of the Aztecs, not loyalty, that kept them under control. The Aztecs ruled their empire by terror. Every so often they would remind the tribes in their empire of their power, by sending out soldiers to punish towns that had been disobedient or disloyal. Any alliances that they made with other cities in the Valley of Mexico were unreliable, too. The Aztecs were not trusted by anyone, so they had to work hard to keep their huge empire functioning smoothly. Aztec troops and merchant caravans traveled great distances to collect tribute, over high mountain passes, through steamy rain forests, and across dry plateaus.

When Cortés moved inland, 30,000 Tlaxcalan warriors attacked the Spanish. They must have been a terrifying sight for the Spanish; they were heavily painted and wore bright feather headdresses as they swung their swords and hurled spears. As they ran toward the Spaniards, they screamed a horrific war cry. But the Tlaxcalans had never seen steel swords, crossbows, and artillery. They were terrified by cavalrymen on horses, too, which they believed to be strange monsters. The Spanish eventually defeated them. They were then surprised when the Tlaxcalans not only surrendered, but also offered to help them fight against the Aztecs.

◀ *A mural showing a battle between the Aztecs and the Tlaxcalans in 1504 CE. The Tlaxcalans are wearing the white and red headdresses. The people of Tlaxcalan were thought to be fairly primitive. They were normally left alone by the Aztecs, unless they needed more victims to sacrifice to the gods. Then, Tlaxcalan towns were attacked, and young men were carried off to their deaths.*

▼ *"The Great Speaker"
was also known as the
magical rainmaker, who
performed the sacrifices
to Tlaloc that brought
rain. Tlaloc was
worshiped at statues
like the one shown here.
He took care of the souls
of men who had died
innocently, by lightning,
drowning, or other
water-related causes.
His priests were said to
scatter drops of water
and to provide gifts of
rain from bags.*

The Emperor and the Palace

"Emperor" is a European word; the Aztecs called their chief leader *Huei Tlatoani*, meaning "Great Speaker." His main work was with the lands of his empire. He made the decisions to go to war, received tribute, and held talks with tribes from all over the country. After being elected, he had to prove he was a suitable leader by taking an army into battle and capturing prisoners for sacrifice.

Montezuma II was the great-nephew of Ahuitzotl. He was elected emperor in 1502 CE. Emperors were elected from among the available "royals" by a group of nobles, priests, and generals. Often brothers were elected, rather than sons of the previous ruler. After election, the new emperor had to spend four days meditating and fasting in the temple of Huitzilopochtli. Rulers of other kingdoms, including even the enemy Tarascans, came to the coronation feast. The emperor was looked on as semidivine. He traveled on a litter carried by four chiefs, and the path where he walked was swept. His palace was huge: one Spanish chronicler wrote, "I walked till I was tired, and never saw the whole of it."

A second great official, Cihuacoatt, meaning "Female Snake," looked after Tenochtitlan. He—this was a man, despite the name—ran the day-to-day affairs of the government. He was chief judge and supervised thousands of officials; he was the modern-day equivalent of a prime minister or president. High priests oversaw the spiritual life of Tenochtitlan and were in charge of the priestly orders. These priests also ran schools for young boys where pupils were taught how to be good citizens and warriors.

Tenochtitlan also had something similar to a civil service, a large bureaucracy of officials, who oversaw the administration of the city.

Most of the people who lived in Tenochtitlan were craftspeople and commoners. Below them were peasants, who worked the fields and kept the Aztecs' agricultural economy going. At the bottom of the social scale were the slaves. In Aztec society, a man's status depended on how successful he was as a warrior. Apart from slaves, all male civilians could be called upon to act as soldiers. During wars, many of them would have to join the army. Warriors who were famed for their fighting skills would enter an order such as the Warriors of the Eagle. They were seen as the Soldiers of the Sun and wore eagle-headed helmets with feathers. Their armor was made of quilted cotton that had been soaked in salt water, to make it tougher. Jaguar or Ocelot Warriors were Soldiers of the Night. Famed for their spying techniques, they wore jaguar-shaped helmets and jaguar-skin body armor.

▲ *An Ocelot Warrior. There were two special groups of Aztec warriors. Both of them were symbolized by a sacred creature. The Ocelot Warriors had to discover the position of the enemy force and find good positions from which to attack. Once this work was done, the Eagle Warriors would charge the enemy, chanting and stamping their feet. If the battle went well, once the commander felt that they had enough enemy captives for sacrifice, the enemy leader would be asked to submit, and the battle would finish.*

The Spaniards may have been horrified by human sacrifice, but they were also astonished by the high level of social organization in Aztec society. Cortés wrote to the King of Spain, "One may well marvel at the orderliness and good government which is everywhere maintained." The Aztecs had a well-organized economy, a ruling class based on ability as well as birth, a court system, and a very strict moral code.

The City of Tenochtitlan

The valley of Mesoamerica was one of the most densely populated regions in the world.

In the valley, Tenochtitlan grew into one of the largest cities in the world. An island of only 7 sq. mi. (18 sq. km), it had a population of at least 80,000 people—maybe even as many as 300,000. It was linked to the mainland by three causeways and ringed by several small towns, such as Tepeyac. The size of Tenochtitlan impressed the first Europeans who saw it, and they liked the orderliness and beauty. There were handsome buildings of carved stone and wood, courtyards brimming with flowers, and beautifully designed canals. One Spanish soldier named Bernal Diaz described seeing Tenochtitlan for the very first time:

"Next morning we came to a broad causeway… And when we saw all those cities and villages built in the water…the great buildings rising from the water, all made of stone, it seemed like an enchanted vision…"

The city was built around a network of canals. Its traders carried their wares in canoes. The sight of hundreds of canoes laden with foodstuffs, crowding the lake and its canals, amazed the Spaniards.

▼ *These are some of the original gardens at Xochimilco, to the south of modern-day Mexico City. What we can see are the remains of the chinampas, or "floating gardens." The willow trees around the edges of the gardens can still be seen today.*

▶ *The map at far right shows where the city of Tenochtitlan was within the Valley of Mexico*

The three main causeways were made of beams of wood perfectly fitted together, although they were built without iron or steel tools. There were two masonry aqueducts.

As the island city in the lake grew, food was needed for more and more people. Rocks and soil were brought by canoe from the mainland, to make more *chinampas*. On these *chinampas*, and on fields around the lake, the Aztecs grew corn, beans, squash, chili peppers, tomatoes, and amaranth. People even built cane and thatch houses on their floating gardens.

The lake had no outlet to the sea, so it could flood or become too salty. To keep the lake water around Tenochtitlan fresh, the Texcocoan king Nezahualcoyotl, built a 10-mi. (16-km)-long dike. It was used to seal off the western lagoon, which was fed by fresh spring water. The city's water came by aqueduct to a place where it was carried away and sold in the streets.

▲ *A painting depicting how the Aztecs built up chinampas out of reeds woven together. Once the reeds had formed a base, like a raft, the soil and plants were put on top to create a garden.*

This poem is about Tenochtitlan: "The city is spread out in circles of jade, radiating flashes of light like quetzal plumes. Beside it the lords are borne in boats: Over them extends a flowery mist."

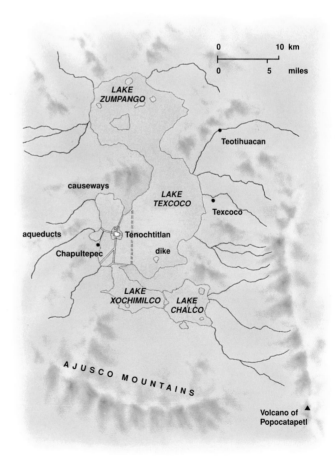

Food

The Spanish conquerors were amazed at the variety of foods and cooking methods used by the Aztecs. Rich people tended to eat more meat and fish, poorer people more vegetables. There was also plenty of fruit on the surrounding hills. The Aztecs who first came to the lake began to include in their diet things like the *axolotl* (a large salamander), tadpoles, water-fly eggs, and a lake algae, pressed into cakes. The rich drank chocolate, which was very expensive. People of all classes had a fermented drink, *octli* (which the Spanish called *pulque*). Four cups, at a feast, was the most an Aztec was allowed to drink. Drunkenness in young people was punishable by death, but older people were allowed to drink octli.

▲ *Carved into the shape of a hare, this cup was used for drinking chocolate. In rich Aztec homes they would drink this, which they called "cacao," mixed with gum and water. Aztecs believed that chocolate made you fall in love and feel happy. They sometimes drank the chocolate through golden straws.*

Markets and City Life

The city had amazingly busy and colorful markets. Each of the four main sections of the city had its local market. There were also two huge ones, in Tenochtitlan and Tlaltelolco, that offered virtually every product that the Aztec empire had to offer. Different sections of the market concentrated on different items. There were sections for vegetables, clothes, hardware, jewelry, meats, and virtually everything you could think of. You could buy nearly anything in Tenochtitlan: richly colored Cholula pottery, chocolate, vanilla, carpenters' copper tools, cigars, and even slaves in cages.

Richer people in Tenochtitlan lived in houses made of stone and stucco. The poorer people made their houses of sun-dried mud bricks, or adobe. All of the houses of Tenochtitlan were whitewashed, whether they were stone or adobe.

Perhaps as many as 60,000 people were engaged in this buying and selling. The markets were so busy, and so important to the smooth running of Tenochtitlan and its community, that special judges were employed to keep trading honest and fair. Thieves were beaten to death; Aztec justice was fair but ferocious. The Aztecs had no coins or money currency. Instead, certain objects were used as a means of exchange: items such as goose-quills filled with gold-dust, cotton mantles, T-shaped strips of copper, and cacao beans.

Tenochtitlan was an unusually clean place. A thousand men swept and washed down the streets every day. Garbage and human waste were carried away in barges. Some barges were moored at the water's edge as floating toilets.

▶ *A reconstruction of the vegetable section of the market at Tenochtitlan. People brought produce from all over the empire to sell here.*

The Temple Precinct

The markets were near the center of Tenochtitlan, but the city center itself was the temple precinct. It was dominated by the two great pyramid temples that stood side by side, their flights of steps like a pair of escalators, facing west. The southern one, painted red and white, was sacred to Huitzilopochtli; the northern one, blue and white, was sacred to Tlaloc, the rain god. In the wet seasons the sun rose behind Tlaloc; in the dry seasons it rose behind Huitzilopochtli. It was up these temple steps—permanently stained red by blood —that captives were hauled to be sacrificed. The sacred precinct was the active industrial center. Its main product was hearts for the gods. Black-robed priests carried incense and led victims to the great stone where they were sacrificed. Every aspect of Aztec life, from crop planting to launching an expedition, required a human sacrifice. Nearby was the *tzompantli*, or the skull rack, in which the skulls of victims were arranged in neat rows.

▼ *This carving represents the skull racks used in Aztec temples. They were to be found near every Aztec temple and held the heads of dead enemy warriors. The heads were pierced through the temples and hung on wooden bars on a wooden frame. There they were left to rot. The rack at Tenochtitlan, which horrified the Spanish invaders, held more than 10,000 rotting heads.*

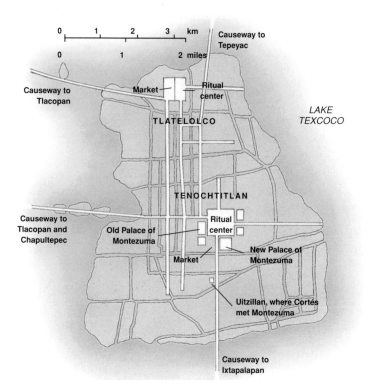

▲ A map of Tenochtitlan showing the canal system that ran within the city and the main roads that led to the causeways.

Next to the *tzompantli* was the ceremonial ball court. Other buildings housed the priests of the Aztecs. Five thousand priests looked after the temple of Huitzilopochtli.

Palaces

Near the temple were the decorated stone palaces of the emperor and of the greatest nobles. They were two stories high, with 50 or more rooms. Montezuma's palace had its own parks and gardens with ponds where swans were kept. Tenochtitlan was a typical city, with taverns, food stalls, barber shops, and parks for relaxation. Many houses had flower gardens, small shaded courtyards and patios, and dikes full of water. The one strange thing for the visitors from Europe was the absence of beasts of burden and carts.

It was not just the Aztec capital that was responsible for the sophistication of Mexican civilization. There were many cities around the lakes in the Valley of Mexico, and many of the peoples spoke the same language as the Aztecs, Nahuatl. Texcoco, on the eastern shore of Lake Texcoco, was a very civilized city and an intellectual center for the area. Its king, Nezahualcoyotl, was a famous philosopher and poet. His speeches are still quoted by modern-day Mexican scholars.

Aztec Religion

The Sun and the Gods

Religion was very important to the Aztecs. They worshiped many ancient gods, but also adopted new ones from different cultures. As more cities paid tribute to Montezuma, and Tenochtitlan filled up with people from all over the country, it became home to the shrines of gods from all over the Aztec world. At one point it was said that there were over 40 major Aztec gods and more than ten lesser ones. Montezuma even allowed Cortés to set up a Christian cross and shrine in one of his temples.

The Aztecs believed that if they did not take part in certain festivals and rituals, the gods might stop the seasons from happening. They also believed that each day they had to prevent the death of the sun, through worship, to be sure that the Earth survived.

The Aztecs thought of themselves as "People of the Sun." Huitzilopochtli was the sun god and the god of war; his name translates as "Hummingbird of the South." Religious life centered around him. This god had fought for his chief position in the sky. When he was born, he had had to go to war with his siblings, the moon and the stars. Every dawn, to allow the sun to rise, Huitzilopochtli reenacted this battle. After his victory, he sent away the moon and the stars; then he traveled in triumph up into the sky. As the sun gradually set, warrior spirits carried him back down to Earth again.

▲ *Ometecuhtli, also called "The Two Lord," was seen as the supremely creative deity of the skies. This god was both male and female. There were no temples built in his honor; his sacred place was the hearth in the homes of the Aztec people. His headdress is decorated with the sign of the milky way, the Star Dragon.*

In the Nahuatl language, the word for heart, *yollott*, comes from the same origin as the word for movement, *ollin*. This may help us to understand why the Aztecs felt that without the sacrificing of human hearts the earth would die, and nothing would ever move on Earth again.

Sacrifices to Huitzilopochtli

Huitzilopochtli needed special food to gather new strength to create each new day. Only the *chalchihuatl*, the blood from human sacrifice, would satisfy him. A peaceful Aztec empire could never have existed. The Aztecs believed that their gods were nourished only on human hearts. So, without the wars, which provided a supply of captives for sacrificing, the gods would go hungry. This would mean that the sun would not rise in the morning and Tenochtitlan would fall from power.

▼ These are the remains of the Great Temple of Tenochtitlan, in modern-day Mexico City. This huge monument had to be built in seven stages and was dedicated to warfare and agriculture. The brazier at the right of the picture, which was used for burning coals during sacrificial ceremonies, represents the god Huitzilopochtli. In the background we can see the buildings of Mexico's modern capital city.

"Wars of Flowers"

To please the gods, the Aztecs needed an endless supply of sacrificial victims. Aztec warriors managed to get captives for sacrifice by waging military campaigns against the Tlaxcalans, an independent state nearby. These ritual combats were called *xochiyaoyotl*, or "Wars of Flowers." They were fought purely to catch prisoner-victims.

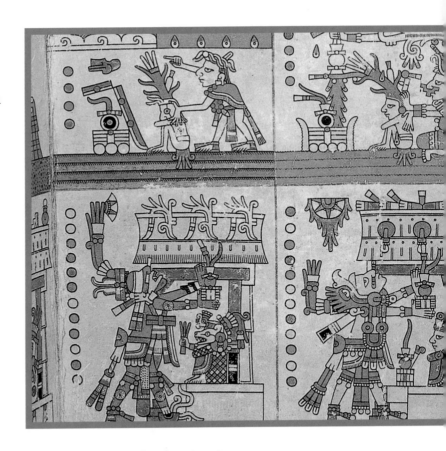

They began after about 1450 CE, during the famine in Mexico; the famine was seen as a sign of the gods' anger at the shortage of sacrificial victims. There was no finer achievement for an Aztec warrior than to take a prisoner, or even to die himself. This Aztec poem expresses the idea very well:

The battlefield is the place:
where one toasts the divine liquor in war,
where are stained red the divine eagles,
where the jaguars howl,
where all kinds of precious stones rain from ornaments,
where wave headdresses rich with fine plumes,
where princes are smashed to bits.
There is nothing like death in war,
nothing like the flowery death
so precious to Him who gives life:
far off I see it: my heart yearns for it.

▲ **The Codex Ferjervary-Mayer *tells the story of the corn plant during the first two years of its life. Corn was one of the most important Aztec crops. Many of their religious ceremonies revolved around the plant. In the first year, the storm goddess pours water over the healthy plant, but in the second year, the plant is not thriving and is being examined by the Lord of the Jewels. The earth is so dry that the stick used for digging, in front of the plant, has broken.***

The Aztecs believed there were thirteen layers of heaven and nine of the underworld. Most of those who died violently went to heaven. For other souls, afterlife was a long journey, with a companion dog, through underworlds of freezing cold or steamy heat. Throughout their journey, they were plagued by the smell of decomposing bodies.

Historians disagree about the number of human sacrifices made in Tenochtitlan. One Spanish writer at the time reported that 80,000 victims were sacrificed when the Great Temple was dedicated in 1487 CE. That probably wouldn't have been possible. However, there is no doubt that local victims from Tenochtitlan were brought up and trained to be "willing" to be sent to their death. The paradise that these "warriors" or victims went to was seen as the highest area of heaven and a reward for their honorable deaths.

◄ *The Aztec warrior was trained to use a range of weapons. He used bows and arrows, spears, and wooden sword-clubs with obsidian (volcanic glass) blades. The other main weapon, the* atlatl, *was a kind of spear from which were propelled feathered poisonous darts or javelins. It could also be used for hunting animals and large fish. The two* atlatls *shown here are carved with scenes of war and sacrifice and are covered with gold. This view shows the groove that the spear fitted into.*

Deities and Festivals

Huitzilopochtli was not the only god that demanded human sacrifice; many other gods expected human hearts to pay them for the gifts they gave the Aztecs. Even children were drowned for Tlaloc the rain god, or their blood was poured into the lake as an offering to him. The victims of the god of fertility, Xipe Totec, were shot with arrows; the falling drops of blood symbolized rain. An exception to the Aztec gods' need for human sacrifice was Quetzalcoatl, the old plumed serpent god. He was also the god of agriculture, education, painting, and music. For Quetzalcoatl, it was enough to sacrifice butterflies, snakes, and birds. People also offered him jade, incense, or tortillas. Tezcatlipoca—whose name meant "Smoking Mirror"—was the god of war. His emblem was a human skull, decorated with a mosaic of turquoise, lignite, and shell. He was the master of life and death and he watched over men through a smoking mirror. This god needed a lot of human hearts. Although sacrifice was very important in Aztec religion, it didn't dominate Aztec life completely. There were joyous festivals with feasting and music and dancing.

The Fifth Sun

The Aztecs lived haunted by a great fear. They believed that they were living under the fifth sun: four earlier suns and their worlds had died, and the fifth would come to an end. It was predicted to happen on a day they called "Four Earthquake," when the world would be destroyed by enormous earthquakes. The prediction said:

"Under this sun there will be earthquakes and hunger, and then our end will come."

▲ *The most important Aztec festivals were linked to the growth of the corn plant. This crop was very important to the survival of the people. In one festival, Tlacaxipeualiztli, a warrior skinned a prisoner alive. He then wore the skin of the victim, as a symbol of the ripening and bursting open of the corn seed. This statue shows Xipe Totec wearing the skin of a prisoner who had been flayed alive.*

The ceremony for the goddess of the young corn plant, Xilonen, required a young woman to die to replace the old corn goddess. The woman chosen was given a headdress of quetzal feathers and her face was painted. Everyone danced and sang alongside her, from twilight to dawn. She would be given octli to drink to numb her senses, and as her dance ended, she was beheaded by a priest, with a gold-handled flint knife.

▼ *This "Calendar Stone" once stood halfway up the Great Pyramid in Tenochtitlan. Using this stone, priests could calculate when to expect solar eclipses. In the center of the stone is the sun god, Tonatiuh, with his tongue hanging out. Around him are the symbols of the earthquake that would end the world. Around them are the signs of the Aztec days of the year.*

Because of this belief, Aztec life involved a degree of hardship; people were in constant fear of the gods and never really knew when the fifth world was about to end. As a result, happiness was always considered to be a little improper. When the fifth world ended, monsters like the Tzitzimitl would hurl themselves on the world and destroy it. This would happen at the end of one of the periods of 52 years in the Aztec calendar. The Aztecs used a solar calendar of 365 days and a sacred calendar of 260 days. The combination of these led to cycles of 52 years. At the end of this cycle, there was an important ritual. The Aztecs broke all their dishes, threw away their old clothes, and put all their fires out. Only when, or if, the new year began again, could the fire be relit. The sign that the world would continue was the appearance, on a mountain top, of the tip of the "Fire-drill" stars (probably what we call "Orion's Belt"). A human victim was sacrificed, and torches carried the new fire down the mountainside to the towns.

Aztec Arts and Crafts

Music, Dance, and Poetry

Every festival had its songs and dances, and there were lots of festivals. New songs were always needed; for weddings, births, victories, deaths, and defeat. Music was important in home life, too; a Spanish friar said, "Each lord had in his house a chapel with composer-singers of dances and songs." The Aztecs wrote poems and songs about everything, including other crafts. This is about goldsmiths:

If he makes a turtle,
it is made like this:
its shell as if it were moving,
its head thrust out seeming to move,
its neck and feet
as if it were stretching them out.

Aztec everyday speech was full of poetry. The language that they spoke, Nahuatl, was a very expressive language, and one that sounded graceful when it was spoken. Aztecs thought of the world itself as a "book": all its flowers, birds, and animals were "painted" into life and would eventually "fade" like painted pages. War was referred to as "The Song of Shields." Anything valuable was described as "Precious Stones," "Gold," "Jade," or "Flowers." Poetry was called "Flowers and Song," and the place where poetry was recited was "The House of Flowers."

▶ *This manuscript shows a native talking to a Spaniard. In codices like this one, characters were often shown with speech scrolls to show that they had authority and were talking about important things.*

Aztec poems and legends were memorized for many generations, just like the epic poems of the Greek Heroic Age. It was only after the Spanish conquest that some of this literature was written down by educated Native Americans or Spanish chroniclers. The Aztecs prized the art of the painter-scribe, the men who painted codices. Only a few Aztec picture books, and no wall paintings, have survived into the twentieth century CE.

One particular festival involved a lot of singing and dancing. The harvest festival, *Ochpaniztli*, was in the first half of September. It was a very joyful ceremony because it meant that the gods had rewarded the people with food, so that life could continue. The main event was the procession of dancing and singing, as the ears of corn were brought in from the fields.

Music for the Gods

To our ears Aztec music—on drums, rasps, flutes, rattles, shells, whistles, and trumpets—might have sounded grim and gloomy. Compared to the music of the European Renaissance, several thousand miles away, it was unsophisticated and jarred the ear. Aztec music, however, was very important. Most of it was for the gods to hear, to persuade them to be generous to their people. And if the gods were to give rain, or send corn, they needed an exact type of music. An Aztec flautist's wrong note would send the wrong signal and offend the gods. If the Aztec drummer missed a beat, the music wouldn't have the same effect, and he might even be executed for causing offense to the gods.

▼ *The* teponaztli, *or two-toned drum, was probably played during religious ceremonies. It is beautifully carved with scenes showing different chiefs at war. All of them are wearing masks of the rain god, Tlaloc.*

Jewelry and Sculpture

The Aztecs were skilled craftspeople in a society that appreciated and encouraged beauty. They were extremely skilled at carving wood, they made exquisite mosaics using precious stones, and they were especially brilliant stone sculptors. The sculptures were often impressive, or even frightening, rather than graceful or beautiful. Famous Aztec sculptures are splendid and handsome, but stern and fearsome, too. Some of the smaller stone sculptures of creatures— double-headed snakes, tortoises, and coyotes—are more elegant and attractive.

Aztec and Mixtec jewelry was admired for its delicacy by the Spanish. One missionary wrote: "They could cast a bird with a movable head, tongue, feet, and hands, and in the hand put a toy so that it appeared to dance with it." Once the Spaniards had shown off their stolen treasures, they melted most of them down.

▼ **This gold nose pendant was made by Mixtecs and is intricately carved into the form of a bearded god wearing a very elaborate head-dress. It would be worn hanging from the cartilage between the nostrils.**

Gold-Working

The art of gold-working was brought to Tenochtitlan by Mixtec craftspeople. Gold was collected locally and then formed into ornaments such as masks, ear and nose ornaments, necklaces, armlets, and anklets. There were professional craftsworkers who were divided into groups, called guilds. They lived together in certain areas within the city. Goldsmiths, feather-workers, and jewelers were called "Toltecs" to show their link with the much-respected civilization of the past. Precious stones were also polished and engraved with designs. These stones were often made into sacred objects and the job of making them was considered to be a religious task.

Pottery

At its peak, the city of Teotihuacan produced pottery that was traded to distant places. This included special bowls and tall, lidded jars in bright orange. Fragments of these can still be found all around Central America. Domestic pottery in ancient Mexico was originally handmade, not made on a wheel. Later, most pottery in Aztec society was mass-produced. Aztec women made their own pottery for use around the home. Some of it was very beautiful, painted in orange and black. A more sophisticated type of pottery was kept for use by noblemen and priests. A lot of it was probably used ceremonially, for drinking *octli* or holding blood. Pottery was used for making ornaments and figurines, whistles used by Aztec dancers to mark time, and *ocarinas*, which are small, pottery wind instruments.

Weaving and Feather-Work

It was only women who did the weaving, and they had a reputation for making very beautiful and intricate patterns. They made and embroidered clothes and sold them in the markets. No examples of this work have survived because it has all rotted over time.

The most respected craftspeople were the *amanteca*, or feather-workers, who lived in the Amantla district. They worked using beautiful feathers, which had been sent to the capital as tribute. With them, they made the brightly colored headdresses and cloaks worn by high-ranking warriors. The feather-workers used cotton thread to tie each feather to a frame made of reed.

▲ *A woman weaving cloth in the same way that Aztec women did hundreds of years ago. The bright colors are made by extracting dyes from different plants in the region.*

Sometimes they pasted feathers to cloth or paper to produce beautiful mosaics. They trimmed the feathers with gold, silver, and precious stones. Many different birds' feathers were used, but Aztecs especially prized the long green feathers of the quetzal bird.

The headdresses worn by Aztec warriors and kings were a symbol, not only of their wealth and power, but also of their strength and authority. Wearing the headdress was a way of showing the enemy how invincible the Aztecs were.

▼ **This fabulous head-dress is said to be one that belonged to Montezuma II. It is made with the feathers of the quetzal bird and trimmed with gold, silver, and turquoise.**

Everyday Life

The Aztec Household

Bigger houses were built of stone, but toward the outskirts of the city they were made of cane, plastered with clay and a thatch of palm leaves. People slept on mats in the corners of the house, with just cotton blankets to keep them warm. All homes had sweat baths in the courtyard of the house. They were used by family members if they were not feeling very well or for women who had just given birth. The baths were similar to modern-day saunas and were regarded as very healthful.

Gardens close to houses were used for growing orchids and peppers. Aztecs liked flowers, and men from noble families would walk through the city carrying small bouquets of flowers. The Aztec diet was varied, and many aspects of it still exist in our diet today. Corn provided cornmeal pancakes, known today as tortillas.

▶ *In the foreground of this mural you can see people bartering for corn. Other traders are weighing goods or handing over money, while slaves roll up great bolts of cloth. Sitting on the chair in the middle of the picture is the magistrate who ruled over proceedings at the market.*

Every morning, people looked out to see if the morning star was in the sky. If it was, they would prick their ears with the spines of a cactus and throw two drops of the blood toward the star, as a gift for Quetzalcoatl. Most Aztecs went to bed after sunset because of the ghosts and bad spirits that they believed were roaming around in the dark.

Other areas of the Aztec diet were more exotic and have not survived into the twentieth century. Mice, voles, frogs, and small snakes were cooked in clay ovens. Armadillos, cooked in their shells, were a tasty meal. Another delicacy was a fat, hairless dog, which was said to be very tender. Mosses and mushrooms were carefully studied by the Aztecs—who made a scientific study of all the plants in their country—and dried, for cooking in stews. Worm cakes and lagoon-weed cheese were two other specialties.

Dress and Appearance

Women wore wraparound skirts tucked into belts and tuniclike blouses. Wealthier women would have little golden or bronze bells sewn all the way along the fringe of their skirts. Their blouses were decorated at the neck and border. Over that they wore a cape with an opening for the head. Most Aztec women had long hair, which they would oil to make it shine. If they were married, they would braid their hair and wrap it with ribbons; otherwise they would wear it loose and well-combed.

Men wore loincloths with elaborately embroidered flaps in front and behind. With that they would wear decorated woven capes that stopped above the knees. If the men were wealthy, they would be allowed to wear feather-work on their capes.

▼ *Pottery stamps were used by the Aztecs for applying face paint. The men painted their faces in bands of black, white, blue, red, or whatever color the occasion required. This varied according to the festival they were attending. They would use these stamps to imprint patterns onto their cheeks.*

Even the clothing in Aztec society was governed by laws. Only the emperor could wear a cloak of turquoise. Warriors of non-noble class could wear long garments only if their legs had battle scars. Breaking the rules might mean punishment by death.

Men wore face paint and headdresses to show their social achievements. It was also fashionable to stain teeth red or black and to have tattoos.

Upbringing and Schooling

Aztec tradition was very strict. Parents had close relationships with their children and brought them up according to a strict regime. By the age of three, both boys and girls had household duties. Self-discipline, cleanliness, courtesy, and obedience were expected. Boys at school had to get up at night and bathe in cold lake water. Punishment was tough: ill-behaved children were held over fires to inhale the fumes of roasting chilies or put outside with no clothes on in the frost.

In 1519 CE, the Aztecs were probably the only people in the world providing free education for boys and girls. At 15 they all went to school—separate schools for boys and girls. The children of the rich and important went to the *calmecac*, to learn the Aztec calendar, rituals, songs, and history. They would then be experts in Aztec history, warfare, astronomy, and agriculture.

Children of non-nobles went to the *telpochcalli*, a military school, where teenage boys learned to be warriors. Sometimes they would even accompany warriors to battle as their squires. The teenage girls in these schools went to a *cuicalco*, a "House of Song," where they learned to sing and dance.

▲ *A picture showing the way Aztec women dressed. The figure with the long hair is a young girl wearing an embroidered cape. The older woman is sitting, grinding corn in the way typical of Aztec women. She is wearing a headdress. Despite the gruesome nature of their religion, the Aztecs loved to wear brightly colored clothing.*

Aztec cotton cloaks were often splendid to look at. One is described by Barnardo de Sahagun: "The cloak was woven with designs that represented seashells, which were made of rabbit hair dyed red on a background of pale blue whirlpools. These designs were framed in blue: one half was light blue, the other half was dark blue; and they also had a border of white feathers. The fringe was of rabbit hair, and its color was red."

Marriage

At the age of about 20, Aztecs got married. A go-between would arrange for a marriage partner, usually someone from the same district, or *calpulli*. Permission from families was needed, as well as from the young man's schoolmasters. Weddings took place at night. The couple sat on a mat in the hearth; the bride's blouse was tied to her new husband's cloak as a sign of union.

Once the couple was married, their relatives would help them build and furnish their home. When they had children, the grandparents would give them presents that would include a jade bead and a green feather—gifts of long life and protection from the gods.

Aztec society was male-dominated, but women received special respect if they died giving birth. It was then said of them that they "did not go into the underworld but into the palace of the sun." They were called "Divine Women"; twilight was their special time of day, and they might appear then to paralyze or frighten passers-by.

▲ *The* **Codex Becker** *shows the marriage of two Mixtecs. The signs above their heads indicate their names. The footprints between them represent the future of the children they will have. The marriage ceremony was accompanied by many speeches; it took half a day to get through them. All the relatives on each side would have their say, and since Nahuatl was such a beautiful language, these speeches were very poetic.*

Classes of Society

Aztec society was also divided into levels. The king and his family formed a large supernoble group. At the top of the Aztec social pyramid after the emperor came the *tecuhtli*, rulers of cities. From their palaces they arranged for tribute to be conveyed to the emperor. They wore amazingly rich clothes, even more splendid than the clothes of the noble class just below them, the *pilli*. The more powerful Tenochtitlan and the emperor became, the more privileged and lavish was the nobles' lifestyle. Only nobles could wear brilliant feathers, gold ornaments, and rich stones. Many nobles rose to their position through being priests. Below the nobles came the free commoners, the *macehualtin*. Below them was a class of laborers for hire, and at the bottom came the slaves. Aztec slavery could be temporary, and it was not inherited. But Aztecs could fall into slavery, for instance, by gambling their freedom away.

The merchants had special ceremonies whenever they made camp each evening. They made offerings to the gods, which they believed helped them on their travels. If they had a successful trip they held a festival. Their homes were often filled with exotic goods that they had gathered from other lands.

▼ This codex shows the patron of merchants, Yacetecuhtli, or "Lord Nose." The cross that he is carrying is the symbol of merchants. This crossroad has the footprints of merchants across it. The other merchant is carrying a fan and a staff and has a cargo of rare quetzal birds on his back.

Traders

The state was dependent not only on tribute, but also on trade. Merchants were a powerful and privileged class. The Aztecs had a special class of long-distance merchants, called *pochteca*. They were treated like noblemen and even had their own law courts. They would go on missions lasting many weeks or months, to bring back luxury goods to Tenochtitlan. On these long journeys they usually traveled at night. They were used as spies, too, and would travel in disguise through enemy territory.

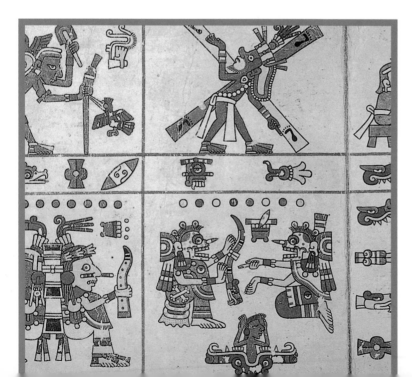

47

The Spanish Invasion

The Conquistadores Arrive

On April 21, 1519 CE, the Spanish adventurer Hernan Cortés landed at San Juan de Ulua, opposite modern Vera Cruz. The Aztecs and their emperor, Montezuma II, were puzzled by these men dressed in iron, who had houses on the sea. "A great mountain has been seen on the waters, moving…without touching the rocks…They saw the craft move without anyone pulling it upon the sea." The emperor and his people knew that there had been bad omens for years: the lake waters had foamed and two-headed men, who vanished when they were looked at, were brought to Montezuma. One Spanish chronicler, Diego Duran, reports Montezuma saying:

"All of us will die at the hands of the gods… It was fated that I should be cast from the throne of my ancestors and leave it in ruins. None of my sons or descendants will restore it or sit on it again."

▼ *Hernando Cortés was born in 1485 CE. He was a devout Catholic and saw his voyage to Mexico as a chance to convert the people to Catholicism. He had a strange, pale face, a small, black beard, and what looked to the Aztecs like painted limbs. These were actually his clothes. He also wore a hat, shaped like the one that Quetzalcoatl wore. So, as far as the Aztecs could see, this really was the god Quetzalcoatl. He had returned to Earth, and he had to be shown respect.*

Donna Marina was the Spanish name for Cortés' companion Indian woman. She was his interpreter. She took a lead in all Cortés' negotiations with the Indians. It is unlikely that Cortés would have conquered Mexico without his companion; it was only through Donna Marina that Cortés enlisted the help of Native Americans such as the Totonacs.

Exchange of Gifts

Montezuma sent the Spaniards gifts, thinking that Cortés might really be Quetzalcoatl, the god-king who had gone into exile more than 500 years earlier, and had promised to return. The estimated time for his arrival was now approaching, according to the Aztec calendar.

When the Spanish expedition landed in Aztec territory, the Aztec official appeared to make the strangers welcome. One of the many gifts offered to them was chocolate. The Spaniards had never seen anything like it before, and one writer says, "When the time came to drink it, the Spaniards were filled with fear." But Montezuma's gifts were a warning. The huge gold disk that he gave them was meant to show the Spaniards that Montezuma was the most powerful emperor in the world. Cortés sent smaller gifts—three shirts and a cup from Italy. Montezuma must have thought that they were Cortés' way of agreeing that the Aztec emperor was stronger than he. Montezuma's spies kept a wary eye on these visitors. His painters recorded everything in detail: Cortés and his captains, ships, sails, horses, cannon and cannonballs, his companion Donna Marina, even two greyhounds.

49

Cortés in Mexico

Cortés was a great diplomat, and shortly after arriving in Mexico he persuaded the Totonacs to revolt against the Aztecs. Then with an army of 1,500 Totonac warriors, he went on to defeat the Tlaxcalans, bitter enemies of the Aztecs. He then made an alliance with them, too. These alliances were some of the reasons that Cortés was able to defeat the Aztecs.

Montezuma worked hard to prevent Cortés from coming nearer and nearer Tenochtitlan, arranging ambushes and attacks by tribute towns and their warriors. The Spanish and the Aztecs fought war differently. The Spanish hid themselves in iron. This looked like cowardice to the Aztec, who showed himself almost naked, painted, and wearing a feather headdress. The Aztecs fought according to rules and arrangements. These "rules," especially the need to take prisoners for sacrifice, weakened them against the Spanish. The Spaniards made "total" war. They gained the Aztecs' trust, then turned on them and killed them. They killed rather than captured. And afterward they destroyed the city of Tenochtitlan and the Aztecs' religious sculptures, burned all the books they could find, tortured the kings, and enslaved the people.

The story of how Cortés came to Tenochtitlan is amazing. He fought endless battles with different cities, winning most of them, keeping his small army intact and alert. His soldiers slept in their armor, with horses saddled and bridled. Having won against many cities, they not only made peace with them, but also seemed to win many of the people they conquered over to their side, ready to fight against Tenochtitlan.

▶ *The difficult landscape through which Cortés and his soldiers passed on their way to Tenochtitlan. Cortés was a determined leader; above all he wanted to see the capital city and its fabulous beauty and wealth. He refused to turn back, even though many of his men wanted to do so.*

▼ *This map shows the route that Cortés took from Vera Cruz to Tenochtitlan. It also shows the retreat to Tlaxcala after the Spanish and their Indian allies were defeated in the battle of Noche Triste.*

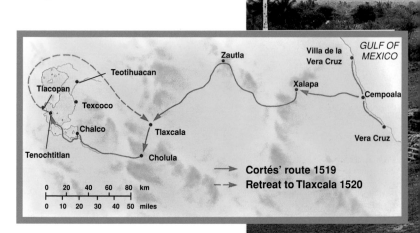

Zautla · Villa de la Vera Cruz · GULF OF MEXICO
Teotihuacan
Tlacopan
Xalapa
Texcoco · Cempoala
Chalco · Tlaxcala
Tenochtitlan · Cholula · Vera Cruz

→ Cortés' route 1519
--→ Retreat to Tlaxcala 1520

0 20 40 60 80 km
0 10 20 30 40 50 miles

Once Montezuma heard of Cortés' victory over the Tlaxcalans, he sent messages to Cortés telling him that it would be best for him to return home; there was little food in Mexico and the journey was hard. All the time he was torn between the desire to defend his city and the fear of attacking what he suspected was a god. To him the appearance of gods marching on Earth seemed real and terrible. He hesitated to destroy Cortés, and this is another reason why the Aztecs were defeated. He did, however, set ambushes and traps for Cortés. But Cortés eluded the traps and traveled on.

▼ *Cortés went to visit the capital of the Totonac empire, Cempoala. He then convinced the Totonacs to fight with him against the Aztecs. He knew that his small army had no chance against the huge Aztec empire; his only way of defeating the Aztecs was with the help of other Indians. When he left Cempoala, he had 1,500 Totonac warriors with him, ready to fight.*

Bartolome de Las Casas was a Spanish priest who saw a massacre in Cholula. He says that the priests and chiefs of Cholula greeted the Spaniards and received them with great respect. Cortés summoned the chiefs and nobles of the city, and without warning took them prisoner. He ordered 6,000 of the natives to squat down like tame sheep. Then they were tied up and butchered.

Cortés in Tenochtitlan

Finally Cortés arrived in Tenochtitlan, having been met outside the city by nobles presenting him with gold necklaces, banners, and precious feather streamers. He stayed, with about 400 men, in halls and great rooms provided by Montezuma. The whole time they were guests of Montezuma, they knew they were never really safe. Any minute might bring the attack and perhaps capture and sacrifice. Cortés felt safe enough to leave Tenochtitlan for a while, to deal with another Spanish expedition that had been sent to arrest him. While he was away, the Spanish soldiers killed unarmed Aztecs dancing in the sacred precinct. Montezuma could not ignore this. Now it was all-out war.

By the time Cortés returned, the tension had built up to the point where Cortés was persuaded to take the Aztec emperor prisoner and keep him hostage.

▼ *A picture showing fighting between Aztecs and Spaniards. The Spanish had guns and full body armor, whereas the Aztecs dressed, not to protect themselves, but to stand out and frighten the enemy; they were equipped with nothing but spears against the Spanish guns.*

While Montezuma was a prisoner-guest, he and Cortés played board games with each other and presented each other with gifts. Cortés had two boats built, to Spanish design but with wood cut by Aztec craftspeople, and on one of these took Montezuma out sailing for a day. It was a strange captivity. It seemed that they respected, and even liked, each other.

Montezuma told his own people he went willingly, that he was a "guest." But once he was imprisoned, he lost the support of his own people. Then, tragically, he died. The soldier Bernal Diaz says that he was killed accidentally. Some people have doubted his story; a later Indian version says that he was strangled. Even before he died, a new *tlatoani* was elected because Montezuma had been losing his power.

The Siege of Noche Triste

The situation between the Aztecs and the Spanish was so tense that Cortés ordered his men to leave the city. One night, the Noche Triste, or "Sad Night," they tried to escape. As many as two-thirds of the Spaniards were killed or dragged off for sacrifice. Cortés was one of the lucky ones; instead of going back to Spain, he gathered a new army together, teaching his Indian allies Spanish military tactics. His force grew to more than 100,000, mainly Indian recruits; many were Tlaxcalans but there were also soldiers from other peoples who were now free of the Aztecs. Cortés marched back into the valley, subduing city after city.

He brought another army to the lake and, with ships built on the lakeside, lay siege to Tenochtitlan in May 1521. Cortés cut the aqueducts that brought fresh water to the city and destroyed the lake area so that there were no food supplies for the Aztecs.

Even so, the Aztecs fought ceaselessly for three months. Their new emperor, Cuauhtemoc, had sworn that he would fight until every Aztec warrior had been killed. However, he was caught trying to escape. When they heard of this, the Aztec warriors stopped fighting and Tenochtitlan finally fell to the Spanish. The fighting had wrecked most of the beautiful city that Cortés had wanted to give to his own emperor.

▲ The siege of Noche Triste. After Montezuma's death, the Aztecs felt free to attack the Spaniards in their city. As the Spaniards tried to flee across the causeways, the Aztecs raced after them. The bodies of dead Spaniards and Aztecs piled up so high in the gaps in the causeways that the escaping Spaniards were able to use them as bridges.

Escape and Defeat

The Aztecs had somehow managed to smuggle out the images of their gods and carry them toward Tula, the city of their Toltec past; and many people tried to follow, to begin their wanderings again. But they were prevented. Young men and the prettier women were taken and branded as Spanish possessions. Most men were set to the task of building a Spanish city on the ruins of Tenochtitlan, the capital of what was to be called "New Spain." The avenging Tlaxcalans, sickened by years of Aztec raiding, killed many survivors, and even tough Spanish soldiers were horrified by their brutality. Cortés received Cuauhtemoc with honor, but three years later executed him. The Aztec empire had crumbled.

▲ The Spanish were infamous for their cruelty toward the Aztecs: "Everywhere," says Sahagun, "the Spaniards were robbing, they were searching for gold... and they took the best-looking women." They enslaved the men, "branding them with a red-hot iron, near the mouth, on the jaw, around the lips..." This codex shows a Spanish soldier terrorizing a young Aztec.

The Aztecs lamented the loss of life and the death of their city in poems:
Broken spears lie in the roads;
we have torn our hair in our grief
The houses are roofless now, and their walls
are red with blood.
Worms are swarming in the streets and plazas,
and the walls are spattered with gore.
The water has turned red, as if it were
dyed, and when we drink of it,
it has the taste of brine...

The End of a Civilization

The end of the Aztecs was also the end of Mesoamerica's 2,500-year-long civilization. In a few years, millions died as a result of war, famine, slavery, and European diseases. Far more damaging than the Spanish cruelty were the germs that they carried with them from Spain. Many different infectious diseases were brought to Mexico by the Spaniards: smallpox, measles, whooping cough, malaria, and influenza. Smallpox swept through the country, killing hundreds of thousands of Indians, who had no resistance to it. By 1600, the Valley of Mexico had lost nearly 80 percent of its people. In 1519 there were perhaps 11 million people in Central Mexico. Just 80 years later, there were only 2,500,000. The Mesoamerican world had been totally devastated.

The Spanish conquerors had come to spread christianity and win souls for the Catholic Church. One friar told people that he had baptized 400,000 Indians in his lifetime! Wherever the victorious Spanish found an Aztec shrine, they would build a church next to it or even on top of it. Although the Aztecs did give up human sacrifice, they continued to worship their ancient gods of nature, and some Mexicans still worship these gods. In their desire to destroy all signs of pagan beliefs, the Spanish destroyed many beautiful statues and burned hundreds of codices. It has been said about Aztec civilization, simply, that "It was murdered."

▲ *This beautiful breastplate, or* Chimalli, *in the form of a shield pierced by arrows, was possibly part of the hoard of treasures that the Spanish took when they left Tenochtitlan.*

55

The Aztec Legacy

Eventually, 300 years after the collapse of the Aztec empire, the descendants of the Spanish settlers and native people won independence from Spain. The country was named Mexico, in memory of the Aztecs. Now, the Mexican flag carries the symbol of Tenochtitlan, the eagle on a cactus.

There are more than 90 million people in Mexico today. The descendants of the Aztecs, now called the Nahua, number over 1,400,000 people. Most of them speak Spanish, but some speak only Nahuatl.

Although the Nahua no longer build pyramids or paint codices, they still weave textiles and celebrate traditional festivals such as the Festival of the Dead. On this day people give presents of edible sugar skulls. Skulls fascinated the Aztec imagination, and this modern custom seems part Aztec and part Christian—as if Christian belief has been tinged by ancient Aztec customs. This festival day falls on the Christian feast of All Saints and All Souls, which shows the fusion between the Aztec and European worlds.

In the mountains of Guatemala, diviners called "daykeepers," using incense and candles, still consult old calendars to figure out the good and bad days and to decide the best times for baptisms, journeys, and marriages.

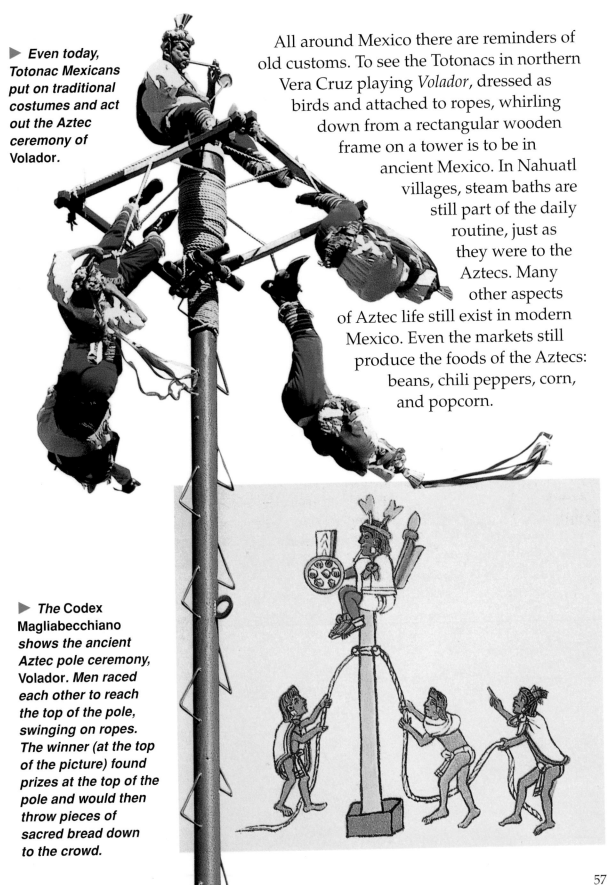

▶ **Even today, Totonac Mexicans put on traditional costumes and act out the Aztec ceremony of Volador.**

All around Mexico there are reminders of old customs. To see the Totonacs in northern Vera Cruz playing *Volador*, dressed as birds and attached to ropes, whirling down from a rectangular wooden frame on a tower is to be in ancient Mexico. In Nahuatl villages, steam baths are still part of the daily routine, just as they were to the Aztecs. Many other aspects of Aztec life still exist in modern Mexico. Even the markets still produce the foods of the Aztecs: beans, chili peppers, corn, and popcorn.

▶ **The Codex Magliabecchiano shows the ancient Aztec pole ceremony, Volador. Men raced each other to reach the top of the pole, swinging on ropes. The winner (at the top of the picture) found prizes at the top of the pole and would then throw pieces of sacred bread down to the crowd.**

Modern Mexico

Many of the ruins across Mexico are being explored and reconstructed. At Tlaltelolco, Tenochtitlan's twin city on Lake Texcoco, a complex of Aztec religious buildings has been dug up, with many of the stone carvings looking as if they had been newly carved. It used to be thought that the Spanish had completely demolished the Tenochtitlan that lay under the present Mexico City. But remains of the great aqueduct into Tenochtitlan exist, and in the last 20 years, parts of the great temple of Huitzilopochtli have also been uncovered.

In 1978, an electricity worker digging in the street in Mexico City found a huge sculpture. It turned out to be the goddess Coyolxauhqui, sister of Huitzilopochtli. Modern buildings were demolished so that digging could take place. Archaeologists then found the base of the great pyramid temple itself. They found many other things: sculptures of Eagle Warriors, jewelry, and hundreds of effigies of Tlaloc, the rain-god.

Tourists are still fascinated by the remains of Aztec culture. New sites are discovered every year, which will be studied and may reveal even more about the Aztecs. On vacations, the people of Mexico City go by the thousands to admire the pyramids built by their ancestors. Tourists arrive to walk along "The Avenue of the Dead" in Teotihuacan, or to marvel at the Toltec Warriors still standing in Tula. The Aztecs knew these places and worshiped at them; they have the feel of the world of the Aztecs. Mexico City's National Museum of Anthropology has the largest collection of ancient American artifacts in the world. It reflects the country's pride in its past.

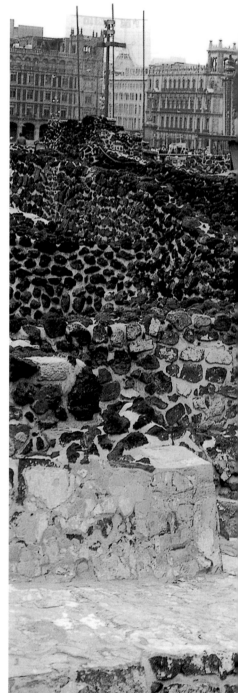

▼ *The excavations of Tenochtitlan are in the center of Mexico City. In the background you can see the city cathedral that was built by Spanish settlers.*

Modern Mexicans can read in Aztec poems the Aztecs' belief that everything has to come to an end, just as their civilization did:

With flowers you write,
Giver of Life.
With songs you give color.
With songs you shade
those who live here on the Earth.

Later you will erase eagles and tigers.
We exist only in your book
while we are here on Earth.

Today, ancient festivals are revived, and dances hundreds of years old are performed again. Some Mexicans who have no Aztec blood even study Nahuatl. The Mexican government encourages interest in the Aztec past, and the people of Mexico are proud of their ancestors and the remarkable civilization that they constructed. Although Mexico today is a very modern country—with new technology, modern cities and towns, and a stable government—in some parts of the country, isolated villages exist where old customs are still followed, and times have hardly changed since even before the Spanish invaded Mexico. In places like this, it feels as if the Aztecs are never very far away.

▼ *A fertility and rain-making festival that is still celebrated in Mexico. Although different clothes are worn and there is no human sacrifice, the people still ask the Jaguar god to send rain in exchange for the sacrifice of human blood. In this ceremony some of the Aztec culture survives.*

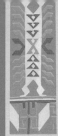

Time Line

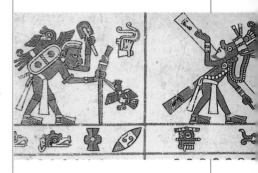

1200 Mixtec civilization grows.
1299 Mexica people arrive in Central Mexico.
1345 Tenochtitlan founded.
1440 Montezuma I becomes emperor.
1440 Growth of Mexica Aztec empire begins.
1460 Ahuitzotl sacrifices 20,000 victims at dedication of temple to Huitzilopochtli.

1519 Cortés leads expedition to Mexico. On November 8, Cortés enters Tenochtitlan.
1520 Death of Montezuma II. On June 30, "Noche Triste," Cortés escapes from Tenochtitlan.
1521 Siege and final fall of Tenochtitlan to Spaniards from April 28 to August 13.

BCE
1000 Olmec culture spreads widely.
400 Olmec culture coming to an end.
200 Beginnings of Mayan culture.
200 Beginnings of Zapotec culture.

CE
100 Beginnings of Zapotec and Totonac culture.
300 Teotihuacan built and becomes a flourishing city.
400 Mayan art becomes highly developed.
600 Date given for the death of Quetzalcoatl.
750 Chichimecs invade and overthrow Teotihuacan.
900 Toltecs set up city of Tula in Valley of Mexico.
1111 Mexica leave Aztlan.
1168 Fall of Toltec capital.

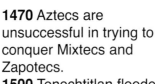

1470 Aztecs are unsuccessful in trying to conquer Mixtecs and Zapotecs.
1500 Tenochtitlan flooded.
1502 Montezuma II comes to the throne.
1504 Cortés leaves Spain.
1511 Spaniards in Cuba.
1517 First Spanish expedition to Mexico.

Glossary

Adobe Unfired mud brick that has been dried in the sun.

Amanteca Craftspeople who worked with feathers to make beautiful head-dresses, battle clothes, and decorations.

Amaranth A nutritious form of grain that was a very important food crop since it ripened before the corn crops were ready for harvesting. A good amaranth crop was important just in case the corn crop failed.

Axin An ointment used by Aztec women for yellowing the skin.

Aztecs Peoples of Central Mexico, descendants of the Mexica.

Calmecac A special school where boys were trained for important positions as priests or leaders.

Calpulli Hereditory clans of the Aztec.

Causeway A kind of bridge used as a road, usually over water: there were several causeways leading to Tenochtitlan.

Chinampas Manmade islets that were used for growing crops.

Codex A precious painted book with the knowledge of the Aztecs painted on the pages and folded in a zigzag fashion.

Conquistadores Spanish conquerors of Mexico in the sixteenth century CE.

Hieroglyphics Sacred writing, often carved in stone and also written and painted in codices. They were stylized pictures used to show objects and ideas.

Macehualtin Free commoners in Aztec society.

Mesoamerica The region that included Central America and large parts of modern-day Mexico.

Mexica The original Aztecs.

Nahuatl The language spoken by the Aztecs as well as some other peoples around the Valley of Mexico.

Nomads Tribes that move from place to place to find land suitable for growing crops.

Obsidian A kind of black, volcanic glass used by the Aztecs for weapons and mirrors. It was a particularly hard substance.

Ocarina Small wind instrument, made of stone or wood and carved into animal shapes.

Octli (called *pulque* by the Spanish) A special, fermented drink.

Ollama A competitive ballgame played by the Aztecs with a heavy ball.

Pipiltin A class of nobles in Aztec society.

Pochteca A special class of traveling traders.

Pyramid A pyramid shaped like a "pyre." Aztec pyramids were temples.

Quetzal bird A bird prized in Aztec times for its long, green tail feathers.

Telpochcalli A neighborhood school where young men learned to be warriors.

Teotihuacan A city to the north of Lake Texcoco. The Aztecs worshiped the city and called it "The City of the Gods."

Teponaztli A wooden gong made into a cylindrical shape.

Texcoco A town near Tenochtitlan; a member of the Triple Alliance.

Tlacopan A city to the west of Tenochtitlan; part of the Triple Alliance.

Tlatoani Meaning "the speaker," or leader; on the pages of codices they are shown with speech scrolls coming from their mouths.

Tlaxcala A city to the east of Tenochtitlan whose citizens were constantly raided by the Aztecs for sacrifice victims.

Toltecs The warlike civilization that dominated Mesoamerica between 99 CE and 1170 CE.

Tribute The "taxes" on objects and manufactured things that cities and towns in the Aztec empire sent to the emperor in Tenochtitlan.

Tzompantli A rack for the skulls of all the victims of sacrifice. These were usually found outside the temples of Tenochtitlan.

"Wars of Flowers" The name given to the raiding parties of warriors, sent out by the Aztecs to seize victims for sacrifice.

Further Reading and Web Sites

Books

The Aztecs: Life in Tenochtitlan
by Matt Doeden
Millbrook Press, 2009

The Aztec and Maya Worlds
by Fiona MacDonald
Rosen Publishing Group, 2009

Hidden World of the Aztec
by Peter Lourie
Boyds Mill Press, 2006

Web Sites

http://library.thinkquest.org/27981/?tqskip=1

http://www.aztecs.mrdonn.org/

Index